45 Things

I've Learned

in 45 Years

By: Ericka Broaddus Johnson

ISBN: 979-8-218-55823-9

Dedication

I am truly Grateful to God for everything that I am able to do, and give thanks to Him for it all. With that said, I am also thankful for my family. There are lots of tough times but, they make the days a little brighter and I love them immensely. And lastly, I have to give a special shout out to my Soror, Celia who quickly rattled off this sounds like another book to me when I originally recited my 45 Things I've Learned in 45 Years at my Birthday Dinner….. I Love You Sis.

Table of Contents

Chapter 1: Be Thankful 1

Chapter 2: Embracing Imperfection 6

Chapter 3: Faith & Spirituality 12

Chapter 4: Relationships and Connections......18

Chapter 5: Self-Discovery and Growth 26

Chapter 6: Health and Wellness 32

Chapter 7: Joy and Gratitude 38

Chapter 8: Personal Insights 44

Chapter 9: Conclusion and Reflections 49

Forward

Welcome to "45 Things I've Learned in 45 Years"—a lighthearted, yet heartfelt collection of lessons learned, moments cherished, and truths discovered over the course of a life that's still unfolding.

If you're reading this, you're probably looking for a good laugh, some inspiration, or maybe even a little comfort. You've come to the right place. This book isn't about perfection—it's about embracing the beautiful mess that life can be. As I reflect on my 45 years, I've come to realize that growth doesn't happen in the absence of mistakes, setbacks, or awkward moments. In fact, those very things have taught me some of the most valuable lessons I now hold dear.

You'll find humor in these pages, but you'll also find truth, love, and vulnerability. From the smallest everyday insights to the bigger, life-changing revelations, every lesson in here has been shaped by my journey and my desire to encourage you to walk confidently in yours. There's no magic formula for life, but there is a whole lot of grace and resilience to be found in the process.

So, sit back, relax, and enjoy this quirky, encouraging, and hopefully thought-provoking ride. You might just walk away with a few laughs, a few 'aha' moments, or a renewed sense of gratitude for the lessons you've already learned—and the ones still ahead.

Let's get started.

— Ericka Broaddus Johnson

Be
Thankful

Chapter 1: Be Thankful

#1 Be Thankful for each day.

There is somebody somewhere that didn't make it to today- Rock it for them!

#2 It's My Birthday Year Y'all!!!

That means I made it to 45. It also means I've made it through a lot of crap to get here (so guess what? You CAN too!!!!!).

#3 Make it a Point to Find Joy Every Day

Finding joy can sometimes be a challenge, especially when negativity seems to be all around us. But here's a little tip from my own life: Start each day by noting one thing you're grateful for, no matter how small it seems. It could be the warmth of your morning coffee, a friendly smile from a stranger, or even the simple pleasure of a sunny day.

For instance, one morning, I found joy in a perfectly bloomed flower in my garden. It wasn't just about the flower itself, but the way it reminded me that even small, everyday things can be beautiful and worth appreciating.

I challenge you to do the same. When you find yourself caught up in negativity, take a moment to pause and identify something positive. Share that joy with others, whether through a kind word, a smile, or simply being present. Your light can make a difference in someone else's day and, in turn, brighten your own.

#4 I Love Each and Every One of You!

Yes, really! It's a bit surprising how easy it can be to extend love and support to a stranger, isn't it? I remember a time when a stranger's kind gesture made my day—it was a simple act, but it left a lasting impression. It made me realize that love and appreciation don't have to be reserved for those closest to us.

So here's a thought: let's make a habit of spreading that love a little further. When you see someone who looks like they could use a kind word or a helping hand, don't hesitate. Sometimes the simplest acts of kindness can have the biggest impact.

And to you, my dear reader, I truly appreciate your support. By picking up this book, you've chosen to share in my journey and reflections, and for that, I am profoundly grateful. Remember, each act of love and support you give, no matter how small, helps to make the world a little brighter.

Chapter 2: Embracing Imperfection

#5 It Is Okay to Make a Mistake

Mistakes are how we grow. The notion that we should be perfect is incorrect and frankly, nonsense. No one who has walked this Earth has been perfect. Even in religious texts, like the Bible, it is mentioned that Jesus was 'tempted,' which implies that he faced challenges and had to overcome them. This shows us that mistakes and struggles are part of the journey.

Instead of just aiming for perfection, focus on learning from your errors. Each mistake is an opportunity to learn and improve. Embrace your imperfections, as they are what make you uniquely human. When you stumble, remember that it's okay to make mistakes. The important part is to learn from them and keep moving forward with a positive mindset.

#6 Sometimes Pain Can Lead You to Beautiful People and Places

This is one of my favorite lessons. I don't enjoy going through pain, but I've often found that it brings unexpected beauty and growth. Painful experiences can lead to profound personal transformations. For example, heartbreak can sometimes lead to discovering new, meaningful relationships. Pain can reveal your inner strength and resilience, helping you set boundaries and understand what you truly value.

It can also push you to explore new interests and hobbies you might never have considered otherwise. Through adversity, you may find beautiful new people, places, and passions that you wouldn't have encountered otherwise.

Embrace the lessons that pain can teach you and trust that it can lead you to something wonderful.

#7 Learn to Ask for Help

Whew, this one was a VERY hard lesson for me. I grew up with the belief that asking for help meant weakness. It wasn't until I became a military spouse, new mom, and stepmom, and faced a deployment, that I learned the importance of asking for help.

I vividly remember a day at Panera Bread with my infant in a carrier. The lady behind me paid for my meal and helped me get to a table. She shared her story and gently encouraged me to ask for and accept help, whether from friends, family, or even professional sitters. This experience taught me that accepting help is not a sign of failure but a way to build support and community. It's okay to lean on others and not have everything under control at all times.

Be Thankful
Y"-all!

#8 Be Willing to Let Some Stuff Go

Let it Go!!! Don't let past hurts clutter your mind or unwanted items clutter your space. Holding onto negative memories, excessive material possessions, or toxic relationships only weighs you down.

I'm working on this myself—decluttering my home and life to make space for more positive things. Letting go is about freeing yourself from things and people that no longer serve you. It's about creating room for growth, peace, and happiness. Sometimes, letting go is the best way to move forward and make space for new, enriching experiences.

Chapter 3: Faith and Spirituality

#9 God is Always There – Sometimes We Just Won't Get Quiet to Listen

We get so caught up in the hustle and bustle of life that we often miss the basics. In the rush of our daily routines, it's easy to overlook the fact that God is constantly present, ready to guide us. God wants to commune with us daily, but sometimes we fail to listen. It's not just in prayer or worship that we find His presence, though—God's essence is all around us. It's in the beauty of nature, the way our bodies are intricately designed, the kindness of strangers on our worst days, and even in the unexpected blessings that show up when we least expect them. These are all examples of God in action, reminding us that He's always there, even when we don't stop to notice.

#10 My Birth Was by Emergency C-Section Because I Was in Trouble– God Meant for Me to Be Here

I was born by emergency C-section because I was in trouble, but I believe it was all part of God's plan for my life. It's humbling to think that from the very beginning, God had a purpose for me—one that I'm still uncovering. I know that there's more for me to discover, but I can see some of the pieces now. One thing I've realized is that my inclination to pour energy into others is a part of that plan. God's plan for me is bigger than I can understand, but I trust that every step, even the difficult ones, are guiding me to something greater. Still not convinced? My son's birth was also an emergency C-section because I was in trouble. Yet, I am still here. How's that for another reinforcement?

#11 Life Can Be Hard

Let's face it—life isn't always easy. Some lessons we need to learn are tough, and some situations we must face just flat-out suck. But here's the thing: the key to getting through it is to keep moving forward. You don't need to take big steps every time. Sometimes progress looks like taking a small step, or even just moving to the side for a bit. The most important thing is to keep your feet moving and trust that forward motion—no matter how slow—still gets you to the other side.

#12 I Love to Experience New Things

Redundancy is boring. Life is not meant to be stuck in a routine, no matter how simple things may get. It's about making the effort to live fully and embrace the adventure in every moment. New experiences are what make life rich, exciting, and full of wonder. Whether it's trying something new, stepping out of your comfort zone, or simply appreciating a new perspective, don't let life pass you by. Take the chance to experience new things and truly LIVE.

#13 God Has a Sense of Humor

If you've ever been going in one direction only to be diverted, then you know exactly what I mean. Sometimes, we think we've got everything figured out, but God has a bigger plan. It's like He's reminding us of His incredible power and sense of humor, gently steering us away from what we thought we wanted to show us something even better. I've learned that sometimes, my plans aren't big enough or detailed enough, and that's when God steps in with a laugh, reminding me to trust His timing and direction.

Chapter 4:

Chapter 4: Relationships and Connections

#14 People Can Disappoint You – But Most Times It's Not Intentional

In today's interconnected world, where we're constantly on social media and the internet, it can feel like everyone is watching. With the constant posts and updates, it's easy to think that when people do something, they're doing it with the intention of offending or hurting you. After all, they know what's going on with you—especially since you posted it on Facebook, right?

In reality, though, most people aren't thinking about you that much. The way social media algorithms work, it's likely that they didn't even see your post. The truth is, people are usually just going about their daily lives, just like you.

They're trying to live their 'best life' too, and sometimes, life just happens.

#15 I Don't Care What They Say, Somebody Somewhere Has Aided You at Some Point

As much as today's society loves to focus on the 'me, me, me' culture, with selfies and the illusion of being self-made, let's get real for a second: Someone, somewhere, has helped you at some point. You didn't birth yourself, and even if you weren't raised by your biological parents, someone had to take care of you as an infant. No one does it alone. We are all interconnected, and whether we acknowledge it or not, we all rely on others.

#16 You Can Love People and They Still Can Get on Your Nerves

Let's be clear: Loving someone doesn't mean they won't test your patience sometimes. You can love people with all your heart, but there will be moments when their quirks or actions make you want to scream. That's part of the package. Love doesn't make someone perfect—it just makes them worth the effort, even when they get on your nerves.

#17 Look at the Person Sitting Next to You. It's Their First Time Doing Life as Well. #StillAVirgin

This one's a reminder that we're all figuring it out as we go. No one has life completely figured out.

Everyone, even the person next to you, is going through their own challenges, facing their own doubts, and trying to navigate their unique path. It's okay to make mistakes along the way, because no one else has the manual either.

#18 Love is Work. Family, friendship, partnership whatever, it's the same.

In case you didn't see the punctuation before the previous sentence, let me emphasize: **PERIOD.** Too many people want love to be all roses and rainbows.

But let me tell you something—it's a verb. Love takes work, patience, understanding, and constant effort. As I like to say, 'Love requires work to produce its worth.' That's an EBJ original quote right there.

#19 Check In With Yourself.

While it's important to put in the work for others, don't forget to check in with yourself. Your well-being is just as critical in the equation. You can't pour from an empty cup. Make sure you're taking care of yourself so that you can take care of those around you. Your physical, mental, and emotional health matter, and they're the foundation for everything else.

4:
Relationships
and Connections

#20 Children Help Improve Your Prayer Life.

Let's be honest—children will humble you in ways you never expected. They'll tell you exactly what they think, whether you're ready to hear it or not. I'll never forget the day my child told me I looked like the 'Walmart version of his grandma.' He wasn't trying to be mean, but he was speaking the truth as he saw it. Kids don't hold back—they'll teach you more than you think, and sometimes, that includes a prayer or two.

#21 "I'm Sorry" Can Heal Many Wounds.

Sometimes, words can be harsh, and other times, they're just necessary. But nothing has the power to heal like a heartfelt 'I'm sorry.' We all mess up, we all make mistakes, and it's important to be able to admit it. An apology doesn't just fix things—it opens the door to forgiveness and healing. So when you've wronged someone, don't be afraid to say it. A sincere 'I'm sorry' can work wonders.

#22 Pay Attention When People Show Up for You.

Not everyone has the luxury of having a strong support system, so when someone shows up for you—whether it's through kind words, a helping hand, or just their presence—don't take it for granted. These people are a gift. They're showing you love, loyalty, and support. Recognize it, appreciate it, and never abuse that love. Not everyone has the privilege of people who truly care for them. If you're lucky enough to have that, cherish it.

Chapter 5:
Self Discovery and Growth

Chapter 5: Self-Discovery and Growth

#23 Driving Slow Is Hard

Literally and figuratively, we all want to get to our destinations quickly. We love the fast lane. But, every now and then, we need to remember to slow down and appreciate the journey. Take time to stop and smell the roses—figuratively, of course, because actual roses don't grow on the highway! And don't forget: that traffic delay could be saving you from something far worse. Embrace those slow moments with gratitude, because sometimes, they are part of a bigger plan.

#24 Try It – You Don't and Won't Know Otherwise

Life can be as boring or as adventurous as you make it. Your attitude and perception are the keys. If you sit on the sidelines, waiting for something to happen, you might miss out on a world of experiences. Be bold, take chances, and live it up! That leads me to…..

#25—Have Fun!

Life's too short to watch others live their best life while you stay stuck in your comfort zone. God made you a bird, so fly!

#26 No is a Whole Sentence

Now, while I encourage you to live life fully, don't get too carried away. Sometimes, you need to exercise restraint. Remember, **'No' is a whole sentence.** It's okay to say no without offering an explanation or justification. Live boldly, but don't be reckless. Tempting fate or testing God is a dangerous game, and we don't want to be looking down saying, 'They should've said no.'

#27 You Cannot Expect Everyone to Be You

This one is key. Not everyone is going to understand your perspective, your actions, or your intentions. You might think, 'I've never done that to anyone,' but sometimes, others will do exactly what you would never do, and it's frustrating. But, you have to remember that not everyone sees the world through your eyes. So, don't get bogged down in expectations. Some things just won't make sense to others, and that's okay.

#28 Sometimes You Need to Be Quiet

Sometimes, silence is the answer. Contrary to popular belief, we weren't made to be 'on' all the time. It's important to take a step back, collect your thoughts, and reflect. Running your mouth nonstop isn't the key to growth or understanding. Sometimes, you need to stop and listen—whether it's to God, to others, or just to the stillness around you. You can't hear what's truly important if you're constantly talking.

#29 You Can Accomplish New Things at 100

Age is just a number. Don't ever let anyone tell you that it's too late to do something new. If you've blinked today, you've done something new. Every day offers a chance to learn, grow, and experience something different. So don't be discouraged by the number of candles on your birthday cake—there's always something new to discover. You can achieve new things at any age.

#30 I like to look nice, but I don't really like to shop.

Case in point: I wanted to look great for my husband's 50th birthday party, but I had zero interest in dealing with the tedious details of my outfit for this surprise event. So, I outsourced "the look," and it was fabulous! Delegation can be a game-changer—you don't have to do everything yourself to achieve the results you want.

Chapter 6:
Heath and Welllnesss

Chapter 6: Health and Wellness

#31 Apparently, Extra Pounds Can Lead to Snoring

At least that's what I've observed from others... and trust me, I'm not exempt! Y'all, let me know about your situations too. It's one of those things we don't often talk about, but extra weight can lead to some *unwanted* side effects. I'm just here to tell you what I've seen in the world around me. If you're snoring, it might not be just the sleep itself—it could be time to pay attention to the extra pounds.

#32 Beets Are Good for You

Okay, I know beets aren't everyone's favorite vegetable, but hear me out—**beets are good for you!** You don't have to love them, but there's no denying the health benefits they bring to the table. Packed with vitamins and minerals, they're a solid choice for anyone trying to eat healthier. You might not want to serve them at every meal, but at least give them a chance.

#33 I Love Food, Music & Pets

Honestly, who doesn't? Food, music, and pets are some of the greatest joys in life. Whether it's a home-cooked meal, a song that lifts your spirits, or cuddling up with your pet, these simple pleasures can make even the toughest day better. It's all about balance—enjoying the little things, staying present, and finding joy in what makes you happy.

#34 Popcorn & wine is a balanced dinner. *"Scandal" taught me that :-).* So, when all else fails and you've had one of those impossible days, just remember—if you can pop a bag of popcorn, you might just be okay.

#35 I Can No Longer Eat Pizza Before Bed

As much as I'd love to indulge, I've learned the hard way: **I can no longer eat pizza before bed.** Unless, of course, I want to flip a coin and gamble with heartburn. Seriously, I used to be able to eat anything and sleep like a baby, but as I've gotten older, my body has become a little more... particular. So now, I choose my midnight snacks wisely!

#36 Travel is a Form of Therapy

Let's circle back to something I consider vital for the soul—**travel.** It's not just a 'trip' or an 'escape.' It's rejuvenation, reflection, and expansion. Traveling gives you the opportunity to recharge your mind and body, learn about new places, and meet people who enrich your life in ways you wouldn't have otherwise experienced. Whether it's the vibrant culture, the stunning landscapes, or the amazing connections, travel has a way of reminding you that there's always something new to discover.

Chapter 6:
Health and Wellness.

#37 Apparently My Taste is Expensive?

Okay, here's a fun tidbit—**apparently my taste is expensive.** At least that's what my mother has always implied, and my husband seems to agree. I won't deny it—I've got a penchant for the finer things.

If you want to tie this to my love of travel, let's just say I've been lucky enough to visit places like Hawaii, Bali, Hong Kong, Jamaica, Aruba, etc. But, I am still working on the Maldives, Malaysia, Tanzania, New Zealand, Canary Islands, and Moorea. Yep, my travel bucket list isn't exactly filled with budget-friendly destinations, but hey, a girl can dream!

Chapter 7:
Joy and Gratitude

Chapter 7: Joy and Gratitude

#38 Beauty is a Matter of Perspective

Beauty is all about perspective. To a pessimist, a half-glass of water might not seem like much, but to someone who's been deprived of water, it could mean everything. We have the choice to view life through a positive or negative lens. The question is—**which person do you want to be?** When we start appreciating the little things, we begin to see beauty everywhere, even in the things we once overlooked.

#39 LOVE. Sometimes This Can Be as Simple as Being a Listening Ear

Love doesn't always have to be about grand gestures or solving problems. Sometimes, the most loving thing we can do for someone is to simply listen. Everyone has moments when they just need to be heard. There's real power in offering someone the space to express themselves without immediately trying to fix everything. Sometimes, that's all they need to feel valued—just someone who's willing to listen.

#40 It's Wonderful to Be Encouraged

When using that listening ear, don't forget to offer encouragement. A kind word or a simple compliment can do wonders for someone's spirit. It's free, it's easy, and it can make someone's day. Encouragement helps people feel seen and appreciated, and it costs us nothing to offer it. all need a little lift sometimes, and being the one to give it can make a huge difference.

#41 A Smile Goes a Long Way

You'd be amazed at how much a smile can brighten someone's day. A smile is such a simple gesture, yet it can be a form of encouragement, especially for someone who might be feeling down. I know because I've been both the recipient and the giver of that smile. It's a small act that can change someone's entire outlook, and it's something we all can give without hesitation.

Chapter 8

Chapter 8: Personal Insights

#42 I Have Amazing People in My Life

As I sat down to reflect before my 45th birthday dinner, I took time to think about the amazing people I've had the pleasure to be connected with. Some are family, some are friends who have become family, but all of them have been divine connections. I am truly grateful for each one.

I often smile when I think about how some of my closest friendships seemed like mere happenstance at first, only to later reveal themselves as exactly what I needed. And yes, not every relationship has been sunshine and roses. Some people— let's be real—can really get on your nerves, and you might question just how much you enjoy interacting with them. I call

these 'sandpaper people.' They might rub you the wrong way, but their turbulence is what helps to smooth us and polish us.

We all encounter them, and they serve a purpose. But overall, my #41 refers to the importance of cherishing the amazing people we keep close to us. They are the true gems.

#43 Be Careful with Your Words

'Forgive and forget' is a phrase we hear often, but let me tell you—**it's a lie.** You don't just 'forget.' As much as we try, our brains catalog everything—memories, events, even words. When someone says something hurtful, the words might be forgiven, but they're not forgotten. And that's okay. Forgiveness isn't about erasing the past; it's about not continuing to crucify someone for their mistakes. So, choose your words wisely. Once they're spoken, they can only be forgiven, not erased.

#44 Love Never Fails

"Love is the most expensive gift you could ever receive. It's not something you can buy or hold onto without effort. Love takes

work, and it requires nurturing to keep it alive. Cherish the love you receive from family, friends, and a spouse. That love is precious, and it's worth working hard to maintain. Remember, **love never fails**, but we do need to tend to it with care, patience, and understanding. It's not always easy, but it's always worth it.

#45 Even in Your Darkest Moments, Someone is Praying for You

Here's a truth to hold close: even in your darkest moments, someone is praying for you. But, and this is important, there's a difference between those who pray for your success and those who prey on your downfall. Be careful who you surround yourself with when you're down. You need people who genuinely want to lift you up, not people who will wallow with you or cheer for your failure. Stay vigilant, stay aware, and be grateful for the real ones who are truly invested in your well-being and success.

Chapter 9:

Chapter 9: Conclusion and Reflections

The experiences I've had in my life have helped shape me into the woman I am today. Admittedly, not all of them felt good at the time. There are chapters I wish I could have skipped—moments of loss, heartache, childhood insecurities, discrimination, and feeling less than. But those very experiences, as difficult as they were, played an important role in molding me.

On the other hand, there have been many victories along the way, too. Looking back, I know that in many ways, I am my ancestors' wildest dreams. I was able to go to school—a privilege my grandmother never had. She was forced to quit school at the 8th grade, but I graduated high school with honors in three years and went on to earn two college degrees.

I've also had the incredible opportunity to work on the trading floor, helping move billions of dollars at a time when those kinds of positions were traditionally held by white males. I served on the Board for my local chamber of commerce, published books, and even had a few years to just figure out life—something none of my ancestors ever had the luxury of doing.

When I say I am grateful and blessed, I don't say it lightly. My heart is full, and I genuinely pray that whoever is reading this gets something from it—whether it's a laugh, a moment of novelty, or a nugget of wisdom. Life is full of ups and downs, and it's all part of the journey. So, whatever stage you're at, remember to embrace the lessons, the people, and the moments that make life worth living.

May you continue to grow, learn, and appreciate the journey, knowing that even in your struggles, there is beauty to be found. And may you always remember that no matter where you are, you are part of a bigger story, and your story matters.

ABOUT THE AUTHOR

Ericka Broaddus Johnson is a vibrant blend of humor, intelligence, and sass with a heart that proudly claims, "I'm a child of God." A firm believer in grace over perfection, she embraces her flaws while striving to reflect God's love in all she does. Ericka is a wife, mother, friend, Soror, and avid traveler with a passion for good food and great music.

A proud native of Richmond, Virginia, and an alum of James Madison University (Go Dukes!), she also holds a Master's in Executive Leadership from Liberty University. With a background in banking, finance, and real estate, Ericka's no-nonsense approach to life and work is matched only by her free-spirited, authentic personality. When you interact with her—whether in person, professionally, or through her writing—you'll experience the real deal: what you see is exactly what you get.